PATRIOTIC

MW00607325

HOW TO
THINK LIKE A
PATRIOTIC
MILLIONAIRE

TAXES

BY MORRIS PEARL
WITH **SAM QUIGLEY, WRITER** AND **JULIE TENINBAUM, DESIGNER**

DEDICATED TO:

My parents, who somehow instilled into me the belief
that I really can do anything.

My sons Adrian and Joshua, of whom I am so proud and
who inspire me to do something so that their generation
can grow up with the opportunities enjoyed by my
generation.

My wife Barbara, who has sustained me through every
crazy adventure

And to Sasha, Sam, Kelsea-Marie, and Erica, who
manage to translate my vague ideas into clear words, and
smile while they are doing it

All rights reserved.
Published by Strong Arm Press
Paid for by the Patriotic Millionaires

ISBN-13: 978-1-947492-08-0

ISBN-10: 194749208X

patrioticmillionaires.org

strongarmpress.com

TABLE OF CONTENTS

Dear Reader,

I've met a lot of millionaires in my life, an occupational hazard of working in politics I guess. Money and power, and power and money – a story as old as civilization itself.

Sometimes the politicians feel like props, they're on stage but not really part of the action. Or puppets, maybe, moving around but controlled by other people. Look behind the curtain and you will see the real story unfold: the battle of the billionaires over what kind of country they want and what they are willing to do to get it.

They're willing to do a lot. We saw Paul Ryan get a $500,000 check for a job well done from the Koch Brothers days after the tax bill passed, and that's just a drop in the bucket. Many of the richest people in this country on both sides of the aisle are willing to spend ungodly amounts of money to promote their own personal vision of what America should be, a vision that always seems to include huge tax breaks for themselves.

Last year, a billionaire called me one day to say he was intrigued by the Patriotic Millionaires and wanted to learn more. We spoke for about 45 minutes and through most of the conversation, he was quite enthusiastic about our work.

Charles Koch, Paul Ryan, and David Koch

But then we got to the carried interest loophole, an egregiously unfair piece of our tax code that benefits a few thousand wealthy fund managers… like him.

"Now, Erica," he mansplained, "every industry has its little benefits in the tax code, you really shouldn't spend so much attention on this one."

Now keep in mind, even with conservative estimates this loophole – that most Americans have never heard of – leaves $1.8 billion on the table to get divided between about 5,000 people in the country. That's about $300,000 per person... in a TAX BREAK. Imagine just how rich you have to be for your tax <u>refund</u> check to be $300,000.

This was a billionaire who is a top (democratic) political donor who just couldn't stand the idea of giving up his special little perk – and he sure as heck wasn't going to join a group of millionaires working together to get rid of his special loophole, no matter how unfair it actually is. By the way, this is the same loophole Donald Trump swore up and down to working people across America that he'd close ("those hedge fund guys are getting away with murder"), and then failed to deliver even as he and his party undertook the most comprehensive rewrite of our tax system in 30 years.

This billionaire I was talking to couldn't bring himself to put his money where his mouth was. He just couldn't throw his hat in the ring and say, okay, I'll go first. He may have good intentions, but how is he really any different from the Koch brothers? They're all fighting for their special piece of the pie – or making "big picture" arguments hoping that no one will notice the money they are tucking into their pockets on the sly. And they're destroying the country.

Needless to say, he declined to join our merry little band of no–more–BS–on–taxes warriors.

Some people think of the carried interest loophole as a litmus test for politicians, and it is. But it's not just a litmus test for the politicians, it's a litmus test for the money people, <u>on both sides.</u> It's a way to easily separate real patriots from people who like to get their picture taken with politicians and be lauded for their "patriotism" while they sell out the country.

If people like David Rubenstein, yet another self–interested billionaire rabidly defending the carried interest loophole, would quit spending their money to buy themselves special breaks in the tax code, maybe we would be able to afford to fix the Washington Monument without his help. And then of course, he wouldn't have had the chance to

David Rubenstein with the Washington Monument

PATRIOTIC MILLIONAIRES

HOW TO THINK LIKE A PATRIOTIC MILLIONAIRE: TAXES

scratch his initials in the marble to say "I was here." Yes, he actually did that. To our monument.

The country's millionaires and billionaires have been looking out for themselves forever, but in the last few decades, they have gotten particularly good at it. Essentially all of the economic gains of the last 20 years have gone to a tiny sliver of the wealthiest Americans, and that's not by accident or divine right, and it certainly isn't because they are "better" than other Americans. It's by design. The wealthy have paid for the ability to stand at the drawing board and map out an economic system that works for them, like a factory specially designed to only deliver the finished product to the people who designed the factory. Not an economy "that works," but one that works "for them."

> *To whom is the donut factory delivering the donuts? That is the real question.*

The next time someone tells you the economy is doing well, the first question you should ask is "for whom?" The economy is doing well for whom? To whom is the donut factory delivering the donuts? That is the real question.

I'd love to get to a time where the headlines read, "Economy Surges, Millionaires Left Behind, Everyone Else Doing Great."

Not all the rich people in this country are like "The Davids" (Koch or Rubenstein). There are some millionaires out there who actually care about the country. They are fighting to make sure millionaires pay higher taxes, that they have less political power and that they be legally required to pay the people who work for them something a person can actually live on? In this book, you will hear from one of them.

I met Morris several years ago, when he began attending a regular policy breakfast series I host in New York. He joined our group early on and for the last three years, he's been working with the Patriotic Millionaires full– time traveling the country, working with grassroots activists, testifying in state houses, and meeting with politicians, and advocating for the type of country most Americans want to live in. They understand that millionaires are not the cause of a robust economy, they're the result of a robust economy. And if they want to continue thriving, they better start making sure the economy works, not just for themselves, but for everyone.

The Patriotic Millionaires organization does endorse specific policy proposals and pieces of legislation, but this book is about more than that. In the wake of the most sweeping change to our tax code in decades, Americans still dont have a clear answer to one of the most fundamental questions at the heart of our democracy: what should we do about taxes?

It's a complicated issue, but it doesn't have to be. This isn't a tax book about numbers, it's about values. What should we as a society encourage or discourage? Who should pay for the things that we decide to do together? What is it going to take to build the kind of country that we want? And what is hiding in the tax code that is screwing over regular people?

You're going to have to find those answers on your own, but I couldn't recommend a better guide than Morris for your journey. He explains, with utter, sometimes brutal honesty, exactly how our country rewards people with wealth and power with even more wealth and power through the tax code. We will leave you to make your own judgments about whether the status quo is working for you.

Enjoy.

Warmly,

Erica Payne
Founder and President
The Patriotic Millionaires

INTRODUCTION

BY MORRIS PEARL

I have had only a few moments of perfect clarity in my life. I'd like to tell you about one of them.

In 2013, just a few years after the 2008 financial crisis, I was part of BlackRock's Financial Markets Advisory Group working for the Greek Central Bank, assessing the capital requirements of the bailouts of the Greek banks. I was on the top floor of a bank building in Athens with about 20 bank executives taking a lunch break, when I glanced out the window and saw a huge crowd of people on the street. For a moment I thought it was a parade, and then I realized it was something between a protest and a riot. As I looked out the window to the heated crowd below, and looked behind me to the well–fed bankers at the table, I wondered if I was actually helping anyone beyond the people having lunch with me.

A few months later, I left a 30 year career on Wall Street to work full time as Chair of the Board of The Patriotic Millionaires. I haven't looked back since.

There was an article in the New Yorker a few months ago about all these millionaires and billionaires building luxury bomb shelters and private islands, high end sanctuaries for the end of days. They're willing to pay millions to live through the collapse of society in comfort, but how many of them have spent that same amount – or anything for that matter – to change the dynamics that are creating that threat in the first place?

Elon Musk wants to build a colony on Mars. Should we build a colony on Mars? Maybe as a scientific exercise, but as an alternative to Earth, absolutely not. That's like abandoning a perfectly good fixer-upper because you are too lazy to do your part during the construction.

A single day's worth of headlines can be enough to give even the most optimistic person doubt that we can find our way forward, but all is not lost. We just have some work to do. And it's abundantly clear that it's going to be much, much harder to do that work if my fellow millionaires and billionaires don't start becoming part of the solution. It's time they quelled their hoarder instincts, and started to do their part.

For the first time in modern history, life expectancy is going down for segments of our population. So—called deaths of despair, deaths related to suicide, drugs, and alcohol, are on the rise, and over 2.5 million Americans are addicted to opioids. Those are early warning signs, the canaries in the coal mine, of a society that needs a serious change. We can't stand by and ignore it any more.

My daughter—in—law is Peruvian, and since she and my son met we have spent a lot of time in Peru. It's beautiful, but it's also profoundly disturbing to live among the people and see them struggle through deep, desperate poverty while the elites of their country huddle with their wealth behind barbed wire fences. I don't want to live in a country like that, with a small number of very rich people and a millions of poor people. But that's what we are headed towards.

I want to challenge my fellow millionaires to get their heads out of the sand. I'd rather fix things than retreat into a gated community with a private security force while the world outside the gates falls apart. You are destroying the country, our country, my country, and I'm not going to stand for it.

There's a Greek proverb that goes, "A society grows great when old men plant trees whose shade they know they will never sit in."

Lately, the old men running our country haven't been planting trees, they've been cutting them down to make room for private golf courses. And yes, sadly, it is still mostly men.

The most irritating part of this whole thing to me is that we could fix the problem, or at least get a really good start on it, relatively easily. It would take some time, and some money, but the solutions are fairly straightforward.

And while I'd like to believe my fellow millionaires will see the light soon, we can't rely on them. Regular Americans – the ones without millions of dollars in investments – can fix our country themselves. The system may be stacked against them at every turn, but at the end of the day they have the power.

They just have to decide how to use it.

That's why I wrote this volume. In these divided times, with noise and spin coming from every corner of Washington and the media, it's hard to know who to trust. Taxes are even worse than most other issues, because not only does everyone have a point they're trying to sell to you, they present it in what seems like the most dense, complicated way possible, it's almost like they want you to be confused...

So what I wanted to do in this volume is to give Americans of every political stripe and no political stripe a clear explanation of how the bill for this country is being divvied up. This isn't meant to be the definitive guide to the entire tax bill – that would take more pages than the entire bill itself (and given that most lawmakers didn't even read the bill before they voted for
it, I'm not going to expect more from you). Instead, I hope it's a clear and reasonably concise explanation of some of the core elements of the tax bill, the places where hard–working Americans are getting particularly screwed.

I've laid out this book from my own personal perspective. I don't know if any two people can ever fully and completely be in sync – and a couple hundred millionaires are likely to have just as many different viewpoints and opinions– but I think it's safe to say that our members, while still enjoying spirited debates about some of the details, are generally in line with the perspective I outline in this book.

My intention with this volume isn't to convince (well, okay, it sort of is), but rather inform. I think when you know the facts, the story will tell itself. Rather than agreeing or disagreeing with my position on these important elements of our country's fiscal dynamic, I hope that you will use this to refine and grow your own perspective.

There are very different worldviews vying for control of the country. Ultimately, the American people have the power to decide which worldview wins, and which direction the nation should take.

Everyone wants to talk about what the tax bill is going to do in the future, but I try to provide some perspective in these pages about what it is doing right now, as you read this. How the bill rewards some things and diminishes others. How it helps certain populations and hurts others. I certainly have my opinion about the merit of those changes, but I'll leave it to you to make the final value judgment.

The recently–passed tax bill makes talking about this clash of worldviews much easier. With control of all three branches of government, the Republican party had a chance to write and pass their very best ideas into law. They passed the massive Tax Cuts and Jobs Act along a party line vote, not compromising on really anything, and attracting no Democratic support at all. That dynamic makes it very easy to see the distinction between the two sides. Or at least to get a really good sense of what kind of tax structure the Republican party and the President wanted to see. They had the power, and they created the new tax system.

So now it is all in black and white, lines and lines of text in a bill that is now the law of the land. You have the power to decide.

Choose wisely, the future of the country depends on it.

Sincerely,

Morris Pearl Chair
The Patriotic Millionaires

SO LET'S TALK TAXES

We all know that we need taxes. No one likes seeing that chunk of their paycheck disappear, but everyone knows that in order for this to be the country that we know and love, we have to pay taxes. When everyone pays their fair share, we are all better off, rich and poor.

We can have spirited disagreements about the proper amount of government spending or how much we should be taxing people overall, but we're all working from a common framework that's held this country (and really civilization as a whole) together through its entire history.

There are many arguments to be made about how high taxes should or should not be, but for the purposes of this volume we're not concerned with the total amount of taxes. We're concerned with how they're divided up.

.

For a long time, disproportionate tax burden has fallen on the middle class, and not on corporations and the wealthy. We've let those with the most money, who not only benefit more from our country's protection and infrastructure but also have the most capacity to contribute, pay less than their fair share. This has led to the rich being richer and the poor and middle class being poorer than we've seen in this country in nearly a century. And in recent years this trend hasn't been slowing down, it's been speeding up. We're creating and perpetuating a permanent underclass in this country like some sort of modern day feudalism.

INCOME INEQUALITY IN THE UNITED STATES, 1910-2010

This graph by John Cassidy of The New Yorker shows that after decades of low income inequality throughout the mid 1900s, the top 10% of Americans now earn more than at any point since before the Great Depression

Ultra-wealthy take more of the pie

This image from the Washington Post shows how the country's share of wealth owned by the top 1% has come at the expense of the bottom 90%. The top 1% now owns nearly twice as much as the bottom 90% combined.

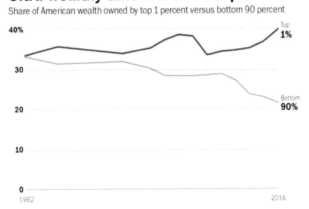

Share of American wealth owned by top 1 percent versus bottom 90 percent

40%

Top
1%

30

20

Bottom
90%

10

0

1962

2016

This photo from the Daily Mail depicts beautiful mansions sitting next to a slum in Mexico, divided by a large wall – the exact kind of society we want to avoid.

This is bad for the poor and middle class (obviously), but over the long run it's bad for the rich too. We don't want to live in a society where we need armed guards and barbed wire fences around our houses because everyone else is so desperately poor. We've seen the lives of the rich in third–world countries, and it's not appealing. We'd gladly pay a higher tax rate if the tradeoff means not living in fear of an armed uprising.

Even on a simpler financial level inequality hurts the rich, particularly business owners.

The American economy is 70% based on consumer demand, and our businesses depend on a thriving middle class to drive that demand. When the majority of Americans don't make enough to support themselves and their families,

"The majority of Americans are worried sick about paying bills, buying a house, accessing health care, and saving something for retirement. We ignore their plight at our peril. No tax cut is worth the social upheaval caused by more tax cuts for the wealthy."
– Karen Stewart,
Patriotic Millionaire

they can't spend money at our businesses, and business owners can't earn money from them . Our businesses don't rely on tax cuts, they rely on demand for the products and services they supply . It's Economics 101 . Unless you're running a payday loan service or a yacht production company, inequality is bad for business .

I want to make something clear. Our members don't want to be taxed more because of some sense of guilt over our wealth. They would be the first to tell you that their view on taxes isn't an entirely selfless one, we just think we'll be personally better off in a more equal country.

As I've told many people who've asked me why I want to pay a higher tax rate – I'm still greedy, I'm just greedy for a different kind of country .

People do have a choice. If you want to live in a tax–free "paradise," there are any number of conflict–ridden third world countries that you could move to. **Anti–tax zealot Grover Norquist, who requires every Republican lawmaker to take a "no new taxes, ever" pledge, once got into a spirited conversation with several members of the Patriotic Millionaire about the merits of the Somali tax code.** Mr. Norquist didn't seem to understand that the reasons that people would rather live in the United States than Somalia have nothing to do with our geography or our weather and everything to do with the protection and services that come from our tax dollars at work (or maybe he does understand it, because despite the higher tax rates here in America I don't see him living in a condo in Mogadishu).

Regardless, having these things means that some resources that could be used for private purposes are instead used for public purposes. **Some money that might be used to buy a gold–plated living room for example, could be used to fund a school, or improve our highway system. Money that might be used to fly on a private jet, could be used to build better airports for everyone.**

Based on the gold–plated living rooms and private jets I'm using as examples, you might be able to see where I'm going with this . When we're talking about who should pay more, we're talking about the rich

WHO SHOULD PAY

Right now in the United States we have a progressive personal income tax system, which means that as you earn more money, that additional money you earn begins to be taxed at a higher rate. So the richer you are, the higher a percentage of your income you pay (up to a maximum of 37% in the new tax bill). This is as opposed to a flat tax, under which everyone pays the exact same percentage of their income regardless of how much money they earn.

"But why," you might ask, "should rich people have to pay higher tax rates than the rest of the country? That flat tax seems much more fair."

Some people do believe that a flat tax is more fair, but we have a progressive tax system for a reason. Consider two things:

First, while a millionaire's overall tax rate may seem high, because of the way our brackets work they still pay the same taxes on the same money as a person making much less. So someone making $100 million dollars a year pays the exact same tax rate on their first $50,000 as someone who only makes $50,000, the millionaire just pays more on their additional income as it moves into the higher tax brackets. **Ask yourself, "Would I rather pay lower taxes if it meant that I take home less money overall?"** Probably not.

The second point is less straightforward, but it's incredibly important. It's called: *The Marginal Utility of Money*

Now, don't get lost here. It may sound like a complicated economics term, but it's actually pretty simple – **the more dollars you have, the less important each additional dollar is to you.**

Say you're a student and you have $100 in your checking account. If someone gives you $100, that's a huge windfall. You've doubled your money and that extra $100 can do a lot for you – pay bills, buy books (well, considering college textbook prices more like one–quarter of a book), or purchase groceries.

On the other hand, that $100 would mean basically nothing to me. A few weeks ago I was reorganizing some stuff and I found a few hundred dollar bills that I put into my camera case when I was traveling in the French West Indies a couple of years ago. Finding that extra couple of hundred dollars did not change my life. There's nothing that I'm not doing for lack of a hundred dollars. It clearly meant so little to me that I didn't even know I had lost a few hundred dollars.

That money means less to me than it does to the student because its "marginal utility," meaning the additional use that money provides to me, is much smaller.

As someone who is living on some millions of dollars in investments, the marginal utility of any additional dollar to me is almost zero. I am almost uncomfortable typing this, because it sounds so obnoxious. But I want you to understand.

The people we want to tax have obnoxious amounts of money – so much so that even if someone handed them an additional $69,000 (the median net worth of every person in America) their life wouldn't change at all.

Please read that sentence again.

Donald Trump has so much money he had to gold plate his living room to spend it. These are people who are so rich they don't even think about money in a practical way anymore, it's all abstract numbers with no effect on their real lives. The money we think millionaires should invest in the country through the tax code would have the same net effect on their life that handing over a single penny would have on anyone else.

Just so you know I'm not alone in my thoughts, at a recent meeting with one of our members this topic came up, and he had a lot to say about it. He went on a… colorful… tirade about rich people who complain about having to pay taxes.

"Millionaires are just a bunch of f*ing crybabies," he railed, "like they're going to die if they have to put some f***ing money on the table. They make me sick." Anonymous Patriotic Millionaire**

I like to hope that they are just misinformed. In some ways this book is for them too. I challenge them to try to read something that lays out the facts, and then ask themselves if this make any sense at all, if it is fair on *any* level. And then look themselves in the mirror and decide what they are going to do about it.

But I digress. Let's look at this idea in effect on taxes.

Take a flat, 5% tax rate increase across the board for all income earners. Someone making $20,000 would be much, much more negatively impacted by this increase than someone making $20 million a year. The millionaire may need to buy a slightly smaller yacht, if he even noticed the difference at all, while the low–wage worker, someone who was almost certainly already struggling to make ends meet, would be devastated. 5% of $20,000 ($1,000) is much less than 5% of $20 million ($1 million), but to the low–wage worker, that money means rent, food, heat, and transportation.
Most Americans do not have an extra thousand dollars. It has a much higher marginal utility than the $1 million does to the millionaire, who already has those things and more covered.

On a side note, even if the marginal utility of those amounts were equal (and they aren't even close) in order to raise the same amount of money in total, you would perhaps mildly inconvenience 1 millionaire, vs. putting the basic stability of 1,000 low–income Americans at

"At a time when those of us in the top one percent are now more one– percentier than ever, it's hard to argue that the problem with the US economy is that the wealthy don't have enough money. We should be paying more in taxes to fund vital national programs, not less."

– Daniel Simon, Patriotic Millionaire

DOES MY RAISE MEAN MY TAXES ARE GOING UP?

Many people have the misconception that earning more means all of your income is going to be taxed more, but that's actually not true. Instead of raising the percentage you pay on all of your income, moving into a higher tax bracket only affects the amount of money you're earning inside that bracket, above what you were earning before. All of your income below that level is still taxed at the same rate as it was before.

So let's say you're earning $49,000 and paying a hypothetical 20% tax rate. You just found out you're getting a raise to $55,000, but the next tax bracket begins at $50,000 with a 30% tax rate. In this higher bracket, rather than paying 30% on all $55,000, you would only pay that rate on the $5,000 inside that higher bracket. The rest of your earnings would still be taxed at the old rate. So your taxes would go from $9,800 to $11,500 and your take home pay would go from $39,200 to $43,500. You are a lot better off with that raise.

THEIR MONEY VS. YOUR SWEAT

Our elected officials may speak eloquently about the nobility of labor and the value of a hard day's work, but money talks louder, and **our tax code is deliberately designed to reward money over work.** It gives an enormous built–in benefit to people who already have money, and are using that money to make more money, rather than those people who are using their skills and time to make money. Here's how. Our tax code has two different rates for two distinct types of earnings: "ordinary" income and "capital gains" income.

ORDINARY INCOME:

The tax that affects most people, "ordinary" income tax, is taken from money earned through labor . You go to work, receive a paycheck, and pay income tax .

CAPITAL GAINS INCOME:

The "capital gains" tax, on the other hand, is a different rate that is paid on money that comes from the sale of an asset . So you buy a stock or real estate, it goes up in value, and you sell it for a profit . That profit is considered a capital gain, and as long as you held that asset for at least a year, you pay the capital gains rate instead of the ordinary income tax rate .

What most people talking about the income tax rate don't mention is that most of the ultra–rich make the vast majority of their money through capital gains, not income. They don't work in the way most Americans work, they live off of their investments. And it's a lucrative path, because the top capital gains rate is barely over half of that paid for ordinary income. That means a billionaire whose investments earn him millions of dollars while he sits around at the beach and goes to fancy cocktail parties pays a lower tax rate on his earnings than almost any working

American. Furthermore, through the magic of stepped up basis (see page 68), the majority of billionaires who inherited their billions, pay no taxes at all on the gains made while their parents or grandparents were alive.

When you look at the rates for capital gains and labor side–by–side, one thing becomes clear – working for your money is a sucker's game. It's far better to make your money work for you.

 VS.

WORKING PERSON	MILLIONAIRE
Works	Sits on a beach sipping Mai Tais
Makes $77,000 in "ordinary" income	Makes $77,000 in "capital gains"
Pays $6,000 in taxes	Pays $0 in taxes

THEIR MONEY VS. YOUR SWEAT: A CASE STUDY

Say that you and your spouse went to work every day last year, putting in 40 hours a week every single week and together you made $77,000 in combined income. You would pay around $6,000 in federal taxes.

Now say, your neighbor bought $500,000 worth of stock on January 1st of this year and then sold it on January 2nd of next year (you need to hold assets for a full year to qualify for the long-term capital gains rate). If it had grown in value to $577,000, an increase of $77,000, based on the current tax code, your neighbor would pay ZERO taxes on that gain. That's right, **zero dollars.**

So just because you and your neighbor made your money in different ways – you with your time and energy and them with their money – you end up $6,000 poorer than your neighbor.

It gets worse from there. Say your neighbor's stocks did really well, and at the end of the year, his $500,000 investment had turned into $900,000. He would again pay no taxes on the first $77,000, and would then pay just 15% on the rest, for a total tax bill of $45,000.

But let's say you and your spouse got new jobs, and you still worked 40 hours a week, but this time you made a total of $400,000 in annual salary. You would owe over $100,000 in income taxes at the end of the year.

So two people make exactly the same amount of money, but one of them works full time all year and the other sits on a beach sipping strawberry daiquiris. As it currently stands, our tax code gives the working earner about a $55,000 tax penalty.

LONG-TERM CAPITAL GAINS RATE	SINGLE TAXPAYERS	MARRIED TAXPAYERS FILING TOGETHER
0%	Up to $38,600	Up to $77,200
15%	$38,600–$425,800	$77,200–$479,000
20%	Over $425,800	Over $479,000

MARGINAL INCOME TAX RATE	SINGLE TAXPAYERS	MARRIED TAXPAYERS FILING TOGETHER
10%	$0–$9,525	$0–$19,050
12%	$9,525–$38,700	$19,050–$77,400
22%	$38,700–$82,500	$77,400–$165,000
24%	$82,500–$157,500	$165,000–$315,000
32%	$157,500–$200,000	$315,000–$400,000
35%	$200,000–$500,000	$400,000–$600,000
37%	Over $500,000	Over $600,000

Here are the current tax brackets and rates for capital gains and labor income. **Feel free to take a look and see how much less in taxes you would be paying if your income came from capital gains instead of labor.**

THE TRUTH ABOUT
TAXES AND INVESTMENT

There is no reason why people who are investors should pay lower tax rates than people who are workers. I hear the argument that investors need extra incentive to invest, but it is just not true. If I have a million dollars and I'm thinking about what to do, I could (to simplify):

Keep my million dollars in cash. At the end of the year I will still have one million dollars, and I will owe no taxes at all.

Invest my million dollars, and make more money (whatever the tax rate is). Even taking taxes and the volatility of the market into consideration, I'm extremely likely to make a significant amount of money from my investment. A higher tax rate may mean I don't make quite as much, but it's still better than making nothing!

THE ONLY LOGICAL CHOICE IS 'B'!

The only tax–related reason not to invest is if I were just so morally opposed to paying taxes that I would rather have no taxes and no profit rather than have most of the profits from the investment. We certainly don't want to discourage people from investing, but rich people are going to invest their money regardless of the tax rate. **They are not going to keep their money in cash under their beds.**

STOP SAYING I'M A JOB CREATOR

It's time we put the tired old "job creators" myth to rest already. Investing is not inherently more valuable than labor. **It's simply not true that investing in the stock market creates jobs.**

I am an investor. I have not actually worked in years. I let my money make me money. Over the past year, do you know how many jobs I've created? Zero (with the possible exception of some of the staff helping to produce this book). The only thing that does create jobs is consumer demand
for products and services that people can make and provide, not my investment dollars.

There are thousands of people employed making iPhones (earning far too little, just $2.50 an hour, but that's another topic for another book) for the 217 million people who bought an iPhone last year. Now, I'm an investor in Apple, to the tune of hundreds of thousands of dollars in Apple stock. But while I benefit from Apple doing well, I certainly don't deserve the credit for those people employed making iPhones. They only have jobs because of the millions of people who want to buy the product they're making.

Demand, not investments, creates jobs.

But what about the initial venture capitalists who funded Apple at its beginning? Back in 1980, Apple sold part of their company for $101 million. Now those shares are worth around $900 billion.

This may seem like a huge deal for the company, but *none of that $900 billion actually went to Apple* (except for the original $101 million). It's all in the hands of those investors. Apple hasn't grown and created jobs because of its increased stock price, it's the other way around.

Apple's stock price increased hugely *because* Apple's business has grown so much. Apple only had that initial $101 million to work with, which it used to hire people and create products that it could sell for a profit, which it then used to hire more people and design new products.

One could argue that those early investors provided the capital that allowed the company to expand and hire people, but keep in mind that the amount of capital gains that they earned had absolutely nothing to do with the money given to Apple to create jobs. **Their profits on that initial investment could have been taxed at 99% and it would have been all the same to Apple.** Also, keep in mind that they made an absolutely insane amount of money. I don't think any early investor in Apple should be worried about taxes no matter what rate they were paying.

> "Without a thriving and healthy middle class, there are no consumers for what any business creates."
>
> – Abigail Disney, Patriotic Millionaire and Disney heiress

The job creator argument is even less applicable when applied to some of the people who benefit most from the reduced capital gains rates, private equity investors. While private equity firms sometimes do come in and transform a company, saving thousands of jobs and earning their investors billions, just as often they buy up a company, sell its assets, and cut costs through massive layoffs, leaving the company in a worse financial situation but with a pumped up stock price. Sometimes they create jobs and sometimes they destroy them (on average companies bought by private equity tend to have more layoffs and lower wages than other companies), but no matter how you view their "creative destruction," it's just not accurate to think that their investments are critical to keeping our workforce employed.

If we want to create jobs, we should be implementing policies that grow the middle class and help bring people up out of poverty so they can participate in the economy. Consumer demand is king. We certainly don't need to be giving huge tax breaks to people who advise the people who invest in companies that may or may not have created any jobs.

Toys 'R' Us was often pointed to as one of the success stories of private equity. For years private equity managers from KKR, Bain, and Vornado (the three funds that took over management of the company in 2004) claimed that they created 62,000 jobs by taking it over.

They need to redo their math.

At the time they claimed the company as a success story, there were 62,000 people employed at Toys 'R' Us, **total**. But before private equity got their hands on the company, it employed 97,000 people. It was in healthy financial shape, with annual earnings of $252 million, cash on hand of $2.1 billion, and outstanding long–term debt of $1.9 billion. Everything was looking great.

Toys 'R' Us plans to close all 800 of its stores as a result of bankruptcy-related restructuring. Photo Credit CNBC

In 2004, private equity firms paid $6.6 billion for Toys 'R' Us (of which $170 million went to 21 executives who negotiated the deal), and promptly closed stores around the country so they could sell the buildings the stores were located in. They then used the money from those sales to pay off some of the billions they borrowed to buy the company.

In 2017, facing $8 billion in debt, Toys 'R' Us filed for bankruptcy. Just this March, it announced that it plans to shut down for good and will close **every single one of its stores**, laying off around 33,000 workers.

So private equity's idea of a success story is firing a third of a company's workforce, giving themselves huge bonuses, and driving a once–profitable company to bankruptcy. I'm not sure the fired workers would have described it as a success, and I certainly don't see why we continue to perpetuate the illusion that these firm create jobs. They create money, mostly for themselves, and often destroy jobs. And by the way, the tax code gives them a huge tax break for doing so (for more detail, check out the "carried interest loophole" on p.55

An Apple store full of customers, whose demand for Apple's products is the reason for the company's success.

Now, there are people who argue that capital gains must be taxed at a lower rate than ordinary income or investment would dry up and the whole economy would collapse and there would be no jobs at all. I suspect that those people either:

Make all their money from capital gains or

Are politicians who get all their campaign contributions from people who make all their money from capital gains.

Those who argue that higher capital gains rates would keep people from investing at all and lead to job losses either don't know about investing or are just trying to convince people that they deserve a tax cut . I'm an investor (and a significant one at that), and I can say with 100% certainty that the tax rate makes no difference whatsoever in my investment strategy . As I wrote earlier, if my tax rate were higher I would still invest in stocks and companies that I think will make me money . I'd just bring home slightly less because of the higher tax . But I wouldn't stop investing, that would be stupid .

It's simple math . Would I rather continue investing and make 70% (or 60% or 50% for that matter) on all the returns on my investments, or would I just stop investing altogether and get to keep 100% of nothing?

Unless the tax rates on investment income went to 100%, I will always make more money investing, regardless of my tax rate.

Opponents of higher capital gains rates (like Keith Rabois, an executive at LinkedIn and PayPal who said he would quit venture capital if the carried interest loophole were closed) may say they're going to pack their toys up and go away, but where are they going to go? Even if they did take their money and go away, there are thousands upon thousands upon thousands upon thousands (I really want to emphasize this point) of other investors who are more than happy to take their place.

It's time to call their bluff.

Keith Rabois, venture capitalist, claims he will walk away from investing (which has earned him hundreds of millions of dollars) if the carried interest loophole is closed.

THE SO-CALLED "TAX CUTS AND JOBS ACT" OF 2017

THE BIGGEST REWRITE OF THE TAX CODE IN DECADES.

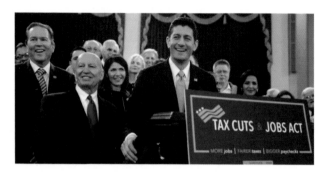

Paul Ryan is joined by dozens of Republican members of Congress to celebrate the passage of the Tax Cuts and Jobs Act. Photo Credit The Atlantic

Now that we have gotten some of the basic ideas down, let's turn to the Tax Cuts and Jobs Act, the Republican party's sweeping rewrite of the American tax code that they passed in December 2017.

As I said in my introduction, this bill makes the job of distinguishing the different sides in the tax debate much easier, because if the tax bill was anything, it was partisan. I don't say that to be critical (although certainly in an ideal world legislation of this magnitude would be something that would attract bipartisan support). I say it because it is a simple fact that the largest rewrite of the country's tax code in the last 30 years passed on a completely party–line vote, with almost unanimous Republican support and completely unanimous Democratic opposition.

With Republicans controlling the House, the Senate, and the White House, they basically got to pass whatever bill they wanted, and they did. So for people trying to make sense of things through all the political spin, it becomes a fairly straightforward exercise. This bill is truly a window into the Republican worldview.

In this next section, I'm going to go through some of the major elements of the bill and explain exactly what it did to the tax code, who benefits, and most importantly, how it affects you. I'll leave it to you to decide how you feel about it.

> *"This tax bill will cause a massive transfer of wealth in our country, moving trillions from the poor and the middle class to the pockets of billionaires and wealthy corporations. It is economically ludicrous."*
> – George Zimmer, Patriotic Millionaire and founder of Men's Wearhouse

MAJOR ELEMENTS OF THE TAX CUTS AND JOBS ACT

REPEAL OF THE AFFORDABLE CARE ACT MANDATE

Reading the header, you may be thinking "hey, why are we talking about health care again? I thought this book was about taxes!" And that is exactly my point.

Republicans in Congress tried over and over throughout 2017 to repeal the Affordable Care Act, but never quite managed to get the votes. All those protesting Americans in congressional offices and town halls around the country probably had something to do with it.

Pictured: protesters marching to save the ACA

Rather than give up, though, they found another way to roll back parts of the ACA by eliminating a key provision through the (seemingly unrelated) tax bill. The provision they eliminated was the individual mandate, which required people to either buy insurance or pay a fine to the IRS. Counterintuitively, the elimination of this "fine" actually saves the government money in the long run by cutting the amount of money it spends on insurance subsidies. Conveniently enough, the repeal of that mandate also freed up money for additional corporate tax cuts.

Through the ACA, the government gives subsidies to people who want to buy insurance, but don't have high enough incomes to afford it. These subsidies range from paying a small fraction of the cost of insurance to covering virtually the entire policy for those at the very lowest end of the income ranges but who aren't quite poor enough to qualify for Medicaid. However, even though the subsidies cover some of their health care costs, for many people insurance is still at the very edges of affordable, or they feel healthy enough that they just don't want to pay for insurance at all.

Without the mandate some of those people will choose not to buy insurance, meaning the government won't be spending money on subsidies for them. But as those people leave, insurance prices will go up (for reasons I will address in a moment), making it unaffordable for millions more.

Those people who want insurance won't be able to buy it, even with subsidies, so they'll go without, allowing the government to keep the money it would otherwise be spending on their insurance.

The issue with private insurance for years has been that some people (young healthy people) are expected to have very low health care costs, meaning that they would be (on average) more profitable per person than older, sicker people for the companies that insure them. But because they are less likely to need insurance, they've been less likely to buy insurance. This gives insurance companies the justification they need to charge everyone else more money to cover costs.

The entire point of the individual mandate was to lower costs for everyone by encouraging healthy people, who might otherwise think they didn't need to buy insurance, to become insured. This expanded the "risk pool", or the total group of people buying insurance, and drove down premiums. By adding young, healthy people to insurance pools, those pools became on average younger and healthier, and the "average" person required less health care, meaning the insurance companies didn't need to charge as much per person to cover their costs.

Repealing the mandate will do the opposite (it goes into effect in 2019). By removing the incentive for younger, healthier people to buy insurance, the insurance marketplace becomes older and sicker, and, in turn, insurance companies will charge more per person. The Congressional Budget Office, Congress' nonpartisan scorekeeper, estimates that as the insurance pool becomes sicker, premiums will spike by around 10%. This will leave millions of Americans facing significantly higher health care costs, a burden that many won't be able to afford.

In fact, the CBO estimates that this repeal will end up causing 13 million fewer Americans to be insured by 2027.

Unfortunately, without insurance people are less likely to get preventative care, they are more likely to defer care they need, and to put it bluntly, they're more likely to die. With 13 million fewer Americans having health insurance, there's no way to ignore it – there's going to a substantial death toll. **Some estimates put that number as high as 10,000 per year.**

It might not be written down in so many words, but the Republican tax bill made the decision that the money the government has been spending on health care would be more valuable if directed towards tax cuts for corporations and the rich. Maybe it's true – maybe the tax cuts will lead to so much growth and prosperity that everyone will end up being better off in the long run. I don't personally think so, but you decide.

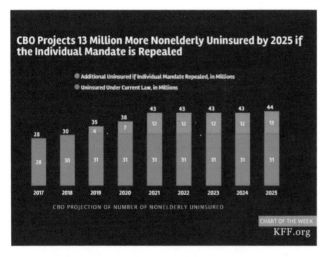

CBO Projects 13 Million More Nonelderly Uninsured by 2025 if the Individual Mandate is Repealed

● Additional Uninsured if Individual Mandate Repealed, in Millions
● Uninsured Under Current Law, in Millions

CBO PROJECTION OF NUMBER OF NONELDERLY UNINSURED

CHART OF THE WEEK
KFF.org

Image credit Henry J Kaiser Family Foundation

Maybe people who are poor don't deserve to live. Maybe our country will be better off with several thousand dead people and a few richer rich people. Maybe, really, rich people are just more important than poor people. Maybe they have more *value*. A few things to consider though, as we weigh the relative value of various members of our nation through the lens of their net worth:

▶ The average nurse in America makes about $72,000 a year.

▶ The average substance abuse counselor makes about $38,000 a year.

▶ The Sackler family, which made its fortune by misleading the public about the danger of OxyContin and other opioids, is worth an estimated $14 billion. Since 1999, over 200,000 Americans have died from opioid-related overdoses. The cost of the opioid epidemic in 2015 alone was over $500 billion

Raymond Sackler with his wife, Beverly.

WHO BRINGS MORE VALUE TO SOCIETY?

CORPORATE TAX CUTS

In the past few years corporate profits have reached record highs, and two–thirds of Americans agree that corporations pay too little in taxes.

The Republican-controlled Congress disagreed. Instead of closing loopholes and putting in place rules to ensure that corporations pay more, they passed a massive corporate tax cut that financially rewards companies for moving money and jobs overseas.

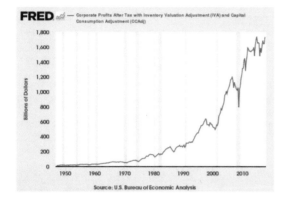

This graph shows how corporate profits have skyrocketed in recent decades, even under a 35% tax rate.
Image Credit to Federal Reserve Bank of St. Louis

The American people may have had a problem with corporations not paying enough in taxes, but according to conservatives, that wasn't the problem at all. The real issue was that the American corporate tax rate was "non–competitive." By that, they meant that there were other countries with a lower tax rate. In their worldview, business people make decisions based only on paying the least taxes – nothing else matters. With that premise, it naturally follows that having the lowest corporate tax rate of any country in the world is necessary in order to ensure prosperity.

Fortunately, the truth is that people choose to build their businesses in the United States of America for many reasons: the most talented people in the world are in America, the most lucrative customer base is in America, and America is a great place to live (among many, many other reasons).

That really is fortunate, because the conservative plan is really to compete in a race to the bottom that the United States can only win by reducing corporate taxes to zero (and that would greatly increase the wealth of the largest corporations).

THE TRUTH ABOUT CORPORATE TAX "COMPETITIVENESS"

The Republican tax bill lowered the corporate tax rate from 35% to 21% in the name of increasing "competitiveness." But was the previous rate really hurting American businesses?

First, let's acknowledge that a 35% corporate tax rate (the rate prior to the passage of the new tax code) was higher than the rate in a lot of other countries. But let's simultaneously agree that the 35% number was basically meaningless. All of the large multinational corporations already have accountants and lawyers who can shift much of their profits to overseas countries with lower tax rates. The only corporations that paid the top statutory rate were small companies. For the very smallest, the new law actually raises their taxes (the current rate is 21% of all profits, it used to be 15% on the first $50,000 with graduated rates that eventually got to 35%).

Those biggest corporations, on the other hand, actually ended up paying, on average, an effective rate of just 14%, which is in fact lower than that of most other developed countries. Because they've been able to avoid paying the full statutory rate, the US government actually takes in less corporate profits than most other developed countries as a percentage of our GDP (2.2% vs 2.9%), leaving more of the bill for running the country to be covered by individuals.

Even without looking at data, it's obvious that American companies aren't struggling to compete internationally. The 9 most valuable companies in the world are all American. They were doing fine without a tax cut.

MULTINATIONAL MONEY GAMES

Multinational corporations have been a particular focus, but what are they really?

"Multinational Corporation" is just a ten-dollar term for a company that conducts business in more than one country.

You might expect that if a company does business in more than one country, that company would pay taxes in more than one country. That would be a reasonable expectation, but the devil is in the details.

Let's say you have a company that buys coffee beans, hires workers, and rents space in the United States to make coffee and sell it to people in the United States. It also buys coffee beans, hires workers, and rents space in Ireland to make coffee and sell it to people in Ireland. In that scenario it's more–or–less straightforward to calculate the profit in the United States and calculate the profit in Ireland. The company can then pay a percentage of its United States profit to the Internal Revenue Service, and also pay a percentage of its Irish profits to the Oifig na gCoimisinéirí Ioncaim (basically the Irish IRS).

Now a large company that serves people coffee might have 13 or 14 thousand stores in the United States and 5 or 6 dozen stores in Ireland, so one might expect that the company would pay a lot of taxes in the United States (at a rate that was around 35% last year, and less this year), and somewhat less taxes on the profits from the sixty or so stores in Ireland (at a 12.5% rate). That would make sense.

But that's not how it works at all.

You see, a lot of large companies have what is called intellectual property. Intellectual property is something like knowledge, a copyright, a patent, or a trademark or basically the right to use some piece of knowledge or information. Intellectual property can be moved easily unlike things like real property, land, buildings, and the like which cannot be moved at all. For example, the right to publish something can be moved trivally. If someone in Australia wanted permission to publish this book, we could (and we would) grant that permission as fast as clicking on "send" on an email.

Now imagine some smart lawyer in Seattle clicking "send" and transferring Starbucks intellectual property – like the company logo – to Starbucks of Ireland (it's more complicated than this but you will get the gist of it) Starbucks of Ireland would then technically own that logo, and Starbucks of the United States would have to send royalty payments to Starbucks of Ireland for the privilege of using it. They can make the royalty payments whatever they want. If they chose to make the royalty payments for the use of that logo large enough, on the books, then they could show no profit in the US and all of their profits in Ireland, even though they sold much more coffee in the US. All of the profit – and therefore the amount that can be taxed – technically belongs to the company that owns the intellectual property (the logo). So Starbucks could end up paying zero taxes in the United States whether the US tax rate is 35% or the current rate of 21%. They would instead pay all their taxes in Ireland (at 12.5%).

> *"The administration still fails to address the tax disadvantages of our domestic companies against their multinational competitors. How does it help to pay only 15% if your larger competition pays 5% or less?"*
>
> – Bill Parks, Patriotic Millionaire and founder of Northwest River Supplies, Inc.

TWO KEY POINTS.

First, by the logic of those advocating for lowering the rate to eliminate these types of "arrangements," if every capable company is going to game the tax system then the only way to "win" is to lower the corporate tax rate to zero.

The corporate tax rate is lower than it was, sure, but the difference between our current rate of 21% and Ireland's rate of 12.5% is still massive when being applied to billions in corporate profits. Do you really think that corporations are going to keep their money in the United States out of the goodness of their hearts, or that they're going to decide it's not worth the trouble to save a couple hundred million dollars? Of course not. The only logical endpoint is a race to the bottom where the American corporate rate is lower than every other country in the world, or financial reform that makes those types of corporate tax gimmicks illegal, or at least ineffective.

Second, this sets small American businesses at a huge competitive disadvantage. A big company can afford to have a few smart lawyers in different countries all around the world. The Mom and Pop's Ice Cream Shop can't afford to hire someone to set up a Mom and Pop's Ice Cream of Ireland affiliate.

REPATRIATION

The big problem with setting up those wonky foreign tax arrangements was that while corporations could transfer as much money as they wanted to the accounts of their affiliates overseas, if they wanted to distribute that money to shareholders in the US, they would have to pay the full American tax rate on it. To avoid paying those taxes, American corporations held over $3.1 trillion in profits in offshore accounts, betting that they would get a chance to bring it back in without paying taxes on it. And they bet right, because the Republican tax bill gave them the chance to bring all of those profits back at less than half the normal tax rate (15.5% versus 35%).

Multinational corporations got hundreds of billions of dollars in tax savings as a reward for what should be tax evasion.

Now, conservatives claim that their policy is bringing about huge investment in the United States because companies are bringing back a stash of cash they have stored overseas. They think that these companies (and it is a lot of big companies) are physically shipping hundred dollar bills and storing them in a big vault in Dublin or someplace. That's just not the case. The money never actually leaves the United States, it is simply invested in US stocks and bonds (they don't want to invest in Euros, that might depreciate against the dollars) but in accounts owned by the overseas affiliates. Yes, the companies are under some restrictions, but the overseas profits *are already invested in the United States*.

Major corporations may claim that by repatriating their money at a lower rate they can create jobs and reward workers, but it's little more than a PR ploy to move public opinion.

Take Apple, which recently announced that it would be repatriating hundreds of billions of dollars in offshore profits at the lower rate. Not content with tax savings of $40 billion (more than double the annual cost of the Children's Health Insurance Program, which covers health care costs for nine million children in low–income families, by the way), Apple CEO Tim Cook wants our praise as well.

In the announcement, Cook claimed that they would be "creating" thousands of new jobs and giving away stock to employees, saying "We have a deep sense of responsibility to give back to our country and the people who help make our success possible."

Rather than comment on that myself, I'll just echo the words of Blaine Garst, one of my fellow Patriotic Millionaires and one of the most influential engineers at Apple for over two decades.

"Tim cooked Apple's books in Ireland to avoid paying $40 billion in taxes, and it worked. Odd to hear how responsible he claims to be to our country and Apple's workers when, in fact, none of that $40 billion is going directly to the employees. Instead, they get about one week's salary in stock grants that they have to wait four years to redeem. Wow, so generous."

THE TERRITORIAL TAX SYSTEM

The way the United States corporate income taxes have always worked (at least until this year) was that corporations paid a percentage of their profits as taxes, with credit for taxes paid to foreign countries. That is the same way it worked for people too. For example, I earned some money in Greece in 2013, so I had to pay a few thousand dollars of income taxes to the Greek government for that year. For my US federal income taxes for that year, I calculated my income taxes as usual, and at the end got a credit for the money paid to the Greek government. The US government still expected me to pay the standard income tax rate (minus the credit), so counting all of the taxes, I paid exactly the same as I would have paid had I had the same earnings without leaving New York.

I had no particular incentive to work in Greece rather than work in New York (well, I did once take off for the weekend to go to the beach in Mykonos, but I meant no *financial* incentive).

It used to be that corporations worked the same way (except that they could defer taxes on foreign profits until those profits were paid to a US parent corporation).

The new tax bill changes that.

Now, corporations actually pay lower taxes rate (about half) on income earned overseas. Imagine that I have a business selling computer systems, and I have an 800 number that people call to get help using the systems. That support is a key part of the value of these system, and about half of my company's costs involve running the telephone support center.

With the new tax system, I can:

1. Open an affiliate in India to provide call center services .

2. Send half of my money to the India affiliate

3. Pay the workers in India (where middle wages range from the equivalent of about $3,500 to about $13,000)

4. And pay a tax rate of only 10 .5% on half of my company profits!

Now, you might ask: why would the US Congress decide to encourage companies to open facilities in other countries?

REASONS:

➤ Some companies have been gaming the system (essentially cheating) for years. Occasionally the government catches them doing something that crosses the line, and complains, and the companies claim that they are in the right, and there is a whole dispute, etc. Congress does not like companies being in disputes with the government, so in general (when Republicans are in charge) they like to change the rules to clarify that whatever the companies are currently doing is legal.

This does not make sense to me. Imagine if you were having a meeting with the managers of your company and one of your managers mentioned having a problem with an employee who overslept frequently and didn't show up to work until 9:30 AM or so. Would your reaction to that be: I know how to fix that problem – let's just change the official start time for the company to 9:30?

➤ The Republicans in charge of the Congress like big powerful companies. Having a few big companies fits into their worldview of the rich get richer. This tax break is very narrowly targeted at a small number of very large companies.

➤ Congress believes that these few large multinational corporations have the ability to move from country to country with the stroke of a pen. According to their worldview, business people make decisions based on minimizing taxes, so they believe that our country must compete with other countries by lowering taxes specifically for the companies who are most able to move. The idea is that by having a lower overall tax rate those companies will be grateful and leave some operations in the United States.

The new system put in place by the Republican tax bill is what economists call a **modified territorial tax system.** In it, not only is the corporate tax rate on overseas profits just half the normal rate (10.5% versus 21%), companies still receive credits for the foreign taxes they pay. So if a corporation earns its profits in a country where the corporate tax rate is above 13.1% (nearly every other country), then it ends up paying **nothing** in US taxes. Not to mention that this change comes even though the bill does almost nothing to stop companies from moving their profits overseas, like the Starbucks example before.

The old system of foreign taxation clearly had its problems, but giving corporations the means to pay virtually no taxes on foreign profits is clearly worse.

For those who don't believe that American corporations should have to pay American taxes on their foreign earnings, there are better options than just shrugging their shoulders in response to corporate tax evasion. One possible solution, promoted by Patriotic Millionaire Bill Parks, is to tax multinational corporations based on their worldwide consolidated profits multiplied by the proportion of their revenue that is generated in the United States. This system, called **Sales Factor Apportionment**, would be fair to both companies that legitimately do have operations in more than one country, and get those companies which are really American but kind of pretending to be somewhere else to pay their fair share.

SENDING AWAY AMERICAN JOBS

Not only does the tax bill encourage corporations to move their money and their corporate headquarters overseas, it actually incentivizes them to move plants and manufacturing facilities to other countries as well. That's right – rather than help bring back American manufacturing, this bill actually gives companies a tax break for moving their factories to other countries.

Under the new law, corporations pay the 10.5% tax on overseas profits, but only on profits above a "routine" rate of return on physical assets (like factories or equipment) it has overseas. Tax jargon aside, this means that the more equipment and factories a company has in other countries, the more tax–free income it can earn.

If that isn't a strong incentive to shut down American factories and move them overseas then I don't know what is.

As you might expect, the benefits of these changes aren't just limited to the wealthy in America. Foreign millionaires with investments in American companies stand to earn quite a bit as well. And by quite a bit, we mean nearly twice as much as the true American middle class, the middle 20% of Americans.

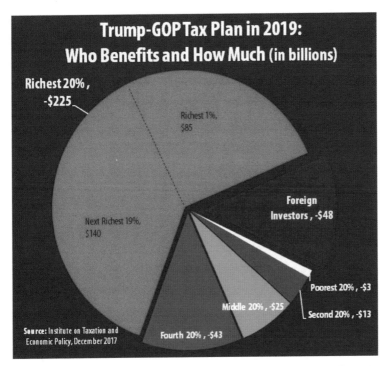

Trump-GOP Tax Plan in 2019:
Who Benefits and How Much (in billions)

Richest 20%, -$225

Richest 1%, $85

Next Richest 19%, $140

Foreign Investors, -$48

Poorest 20%, -$3

Second 20%, -$13

Middle 20%, -$25

Fourth 20%, -$43

Source: Institute on Taxation and Economic Policy, December 2017

As this chart shows, foreign investors gain nearly twice as much from the Republican tax bill as the middle 20% of Americans, and actually earn more than the bottom 60% of Americans combined.

"The administration makes the preposterous claim that this tax cut will 'put people back to work,' but business owners can just as easily use this windfall to automate their factories or open foreign subsidiaries. And the American people will be the losers."

– Patricia Martone, Patriotic Millionaire

LOWERING THE CORPORATE TAX RATE DOES NOT CREATE JOBS

We've already seen companies like Walmart and Kimberly–Clark shut down stores and lay off workers in the aftermath of receiving massive corporation tax cuts, but how do those companies compare with others? Are they rare standouts, or are corporate tax cuts not really the job creators their supporters claim they are?

To determine the link between corporate tax rates and job creation, a recent report by the Institute for Policy Studies (IPS) looked at the job creation records of the 92 publicly held US corporations that reported a US profit every year from 2008 through 2015 and paid less than a 20 percent earnings in federal income tax. Did the reduced tax rates enjoyed by these 92 companies actually lead to greater employment? The data compiled by IPS gives a definitive answer.

No, corporate tax breaks do not encourage job creation.

The average employment growth rate from 2008 to 2016 for all US private sector firms was 6 percent. The employment growth rate for the 92 most consistently profitable tax–dodging firms? Almost negative 1 percent.

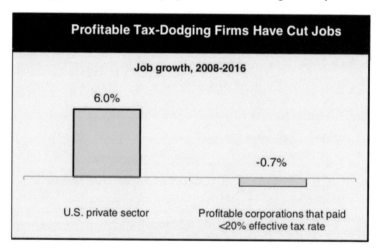

According to proponents of corporate tax cuts as an economic stimulus, these firms should have increased their workforce much more than other corporations that paid higher tax rates, but not only did they not reach the private sector average, *they lost jobs overall.* More than half of the companies studied, 48 out of 92, cut jobs in the given time frame, downsizing by a combined total of 483,000 jobs.

One example, AT&T, is particularly noteworthy because its CEO Randall Stephenson was one of corporate America's biggest cheerleaders for corporate tax cuts.

Stephenson promised that cutting corporate tax rates would lead to huge job growth because the correlation between lower corporate taxes and more jobs was "very, very tight."

(AT&T CEO Randall Stephenson)

Well, according to the Institute on Taxation and Economic Policy, Stephenson's AT&T paid just an 8% tax rate between 2008 and 2015 by using a variety of loopholes and tax breaks. That's significantly below the standard 35%, so AT&T must have created tons of jobs, right? Wrong. The company actually cut nearly 80,000 jobs in that same time frame, despite having the funds to make nearly $34 billion in stock buybacks, a move that surely inflated Stephenson's net worth by quite a bit (he's made over $80 million in five years as the head of AT&T).

SO IF CORPORATE TAX CUTS DON'T LEAD TO JOB OR WAGE GROWTH, WHO BENEFITS?

This answer is clear: CEOs and stockholders.

Average CEO pay among the 92 firms rose 18 percent, to $13.4 million in real terms, between 2008 and 2016, compared to a 13 percent increase among S&P 500 CEOs. US private sector worker pay increased by only 4 percent during this period.

CEOs at the 48 job–slashing companies within the 92–firm sample pocketed even larger paychecks. In 2016 they made $14.9 million on average, 14 percent more than the $13.1 million for typical S&P 500 CEOs.

Many of the firms funneled tax savings into stock buybacks, a financial maneuver that inflates the value of executive stock–based pay. On average, the top 10 job–cutters in the sample each spent $45 billion over the last nine years repurchasing their own stock, six times as much as the S&P 500 corporate average.

This is unsurprising to anyone who's tracked corporate responses to last year's bill. While some corporations have given raises or bonuses, the amount given to workers is dwarfed by the hundreds of billions of dollars that have been spent on stock buybacks. It took less than two months in 2018 for companies to announce over $200 billion in share buybacks, more than double the amount from the same period in 2017.

It actually makes sense that wages haven't increased more, because corporate taxes are a percentage of income, and wages and salaries and bonuses are deducted from income. If any company thought that they could make more money by paying more, they had an incentive to do that already. If a company in the 35% tax bracket pays someone an additional dollar, it only costs them 65 cents. If a company in the 21% tax bracket pays someone an additional dollar, the cost to that company is 79 cents. The new tax bill actually gives companies less of an incentive to raise wages.

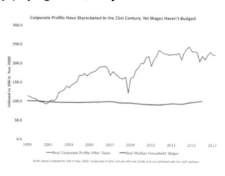

As corporate profits have risen, worker wages have stayed flat

PASS THROUGHS

We've heard "small businesses are the backbone of our economy" from politicians so often that it's become almost a cliché, but in many ways, it's very true. Most businesses – about 95% according the **Brookings Institution** – are not classified as what we normally think of as corporations, or "C–corporations," but are instead registered as "pass– throughs." Instead of paying the corporate tax rate as C–corporations do, pass–through businesses allow their income to "pass through" to their owners to be taxed at the personal income tax rate instead of the corporate tax rate.

The Republican tax bill allows pass–through owners to deduct 20% of their business income from their taxes. So say you ran a pass through that brought in $1 million in income. Rather than pay taxes on all $1 million, you only have to pay taxes on $800,000 of it.

That's a *huge* break for the owners of these pass throughs.

The Republicans gave this cut to pass throughs in the name of helping small businesses and creating jobs, but does cutting pass through rates really help small businesses create jobs? It's a hard question to answer, because like squares and rectangles, virtually every small business is a pass through, but not every pass through is a small business.

Many pass throughs are just legal frameworks that the ultra–wealthy use to avoid taxes.

They're not really businesses, they're just pieces of paper that say this rich person is working as a business and not an individual, and should therefore be taxed like one.

In fact, according to the Department of Treasury, less than half of all people who claim pass through business income actually conduct normal business activity at all. Of those who do, the vast majority are self–employed, with no employees. Only 10% of people claiming pass through income were actually small business employers.

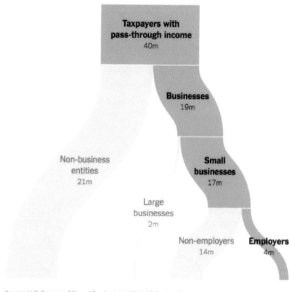

Taxpayers with pass-through income
40m

Businesses
19m

Non-business entities
21m

Small businesses
17m

Large businesses
2m

Non-employers
14m

Employers
4m

Source: U.S. Treasury, Office of Tax Analysis, 2014 I.R.S. data | Note: Numbers may not add up because of rounding.

This graphic from the New York Times depicts what exactly we're talking about when we talk about pass-throughs. As you can see, small business employers make up an exceptionally small fraction of the total pass-throughs in America.

Just to make it clear who the tax bill is supposed to be helping, the bill actually prohibits many small businesses from taking advantage of this rule. Professional service businesses, like lawyers, doctors, and accountants, all of whom frequently employ many people, cannot make full use of this deduction. These professionals are certainly well off as a general group, but their wealth is dwarfed by that of the ultra-wealthy who use pass throughs in real estate and other industries, and who are still allowed to take advantage of this tax break despite employing no one.

Simply put, a deduction for pass through businesses is not going to create jobs.

If we want to help small businesses create jobs, we could give out tax credits for hiring people, or do any number of other things that don't involve giving away billions to wealthy individuals who have the means to funnel their income through pass–throughs.

Really, the tax rate has little influence on hiring anyway.

Since our income tax is based on a percentage of income, if hiring someone will increase the owner's income, it will increase the owner's income at any tax rate. If you believe hiring an additional employee means you'll earn more money, you're going to do it regardless of the tax rate on that profit you're earning. With a higher tax rate you may only earn $50,000 more dollars instead of $60,000, but that's still an extra
$50,000 dollars. Likewise, if you believe hiring another employee would be an expense that wouldn't help you earn more money, you're not going to do it no matter what your tax rate is.

The whole premise of the Republican argument is that business owners first decide how much money they want to make, then they see how much revenue they have, then the difference between those two can be used to hire people. Things may work that way in a congressional office where they have a fixed staffing budget that has no particular connection to the work that needs to be done. Anyone who has actually run a business, on the other hand, can explain that a business person first gets revenue, then pays whatever expenses need to be paid to generate that revenue, and then gets to keep whatever is left. If an expense (like taxes) goes down, the business owner gets richer; he or she does not look for another expense (like wages) to go up in order to prevent the profit from increasing beyond some ordained level.

CARRIED INTEREST LOOPHOLE

The carried interest tax loophole is the poster child for the corrupting influence of money in politics. This is exactly what I meant in my introduction when I said that the rich in America need to start being part of the solution, not the problem. Because with the carried interest loophole, **the political influence of a few wealthy fund managers is the problem**. The carried interest loophole is so absurd that politicians on both sides of the aisle agree that it should be closed, but it's been kept open because of the vast sums of money spent to preserve it.

The carried interest loophole allows private equity and hedge fund managers to mischaracterize their earnings as capital gains rather than income. By asserting a "partnership" with their investors, they claim that their earnings should be classified as capital gains instead of income because they're investing their time and expertise into the firm. This lets them cut their tax bill nearly in half by using the much lower capital gains tax rate, just 20 percent, rather than the top income tax rate of 37 percent. These fund managers are some of the wealthiest people in the world, some earning hundreds of millions of dollars a year, yet they pay a lower tax rate than their secretaries or the janitors who clean their offices.

The capital gains tax rate is significantly lower than the income tax rate for a reason – the government believes that by incentivizing investment and risk–taking, it will spur growth. We can argue about whether that's actually a reasonable policy (I happen to think it isn't), but if we're operating within the current law then we should follow the tax code. Fund managers invest no money of their own and take on no risk, they are simply managing the investments of others.

This should disqualify them from claiming their earnings as capital gains.

But, the fund managers claim, they're investing their time and their expertise, and they earn nothing in carried interest if the fund doesn't make money. Doesn't that count as investment and risk, to qualify their earnings as capital gains?

It's telling that their arguments in favor of special treatment reveal how utterly normal the private–equity compensation structure really is.

First of all, the investment of time and expertise in exchange for money is quite literally the definition of employment.

Second, it's important to note that fund managers typically earn a set percentage of a fund's total investments each year no matter what, which is taxed as income. If the fund makes a profit, they then take an additional percentage of that profit for themselves. That additional cut is what we call carried interest, which is taxed at the capital gains rate. If that earnings structure sounds familiar, that's because it is. Millions of people in thousands of industries get bonuses for performance, and virtually all are taxed as income. **Why should carried interest be any different?**

When a car salesman earns a commission for selling cars, that's considered income. That salesman is managing the sale of someone else's capital investments, the dealership's cars, but because he's operating out of a suburban car lot instead of a high–rise in Manhattan, his earnings face the standard tax rate. It's special treatment for a few thousand millionaires, and unlike some other loopholes that may be justified on the grounds of job creation, the carried interest loophole helps no one but the fund managers themselves.

Keeping the loophole open doesn't help investors, because investors don't earn carried interest. Anyone with money invested in a private–equity fund would still pay the preferential capital gains rate on their earnings, and rightly so. Closing the loophole would only affect the fund managers' taxes on the fees they earn. And in an industry as tightly competitive as private equity, the idea that funds would simply increase their fees to compensate is ridiculous.

There are only about 3,000 to 5,000 fund managers in the US who benefit from carried interest, but because they earn so much per year, the amount of tax revenue lost through this loophole is staggering.

Split between just a few thousand fund managers, they save an estimated $1.8 to $18 billion each year.

This is an astronomical amount of money to be split between so few people, and by closing the loophole we could raise significant funds for important government programs, all from millionaires who have avoided paying the proper tax rate for decades.

The carried interest loophole is so egregious that it is one of the few tax policies that Democrats and Republicans can agree on. During his 2016 campaign Donald Trump spoke out many times in support of closing the carried interest loophole, saying the managers taking advantage of it were **"getting away with murder."**

Closing the loophole should have been an easy opportunity for our leaders in Washington to show that bipartisanship and cooperation were still possible, but because of a dedicated lobbying effort on behalf of the private–equity industry, the Republican tax bill didn't just fail to close the loophole.

It actually made it worse.

Previously, the carried interest loophole existed only because of a convoluted misinterpretation of a piece of the tax code, an interpretation that the IRS could have technically reconsidered at any time. In altering the loophole, the bill actually codified it into the tax code, giving it a specific legal grounding that it had previously lacked, by allowing a special tax break for investment managers if their clients hold assets for three years or more.

The administration claims that requiring assets to be held for three years was a huge change that basically closes the loophole, but it actually affects a small portion of carried interest income, and the fundamental unfairness is exactly the same. The vast majority of fund managers who take advantage of the carried interest loophole hold their assets for more than three years anyway, so this change is effectively worthless. Already, only 24.3% of private equity deals in the US since 2000 would have been affected by this change, and that number is surely going to drop as funds change their behavior to account for the new law. If they're incentivized to the tune of hundreds of millions of dollars to hold assets for another year, they're going to hold assets for another year.

And this entirely inadequate change may not even hold up. An "error" in the bill left a loophole within this loophole that now allows fund managers to incorporate as pass throughs and avoid the three year waiting period completely.

The carried interest loophole is as open as ever, thanks to the lobbying efforts of a wide bipartisan coalition of people with a vested interest in ensuring private equity fund managers continue to make a ton of money. From Mike Sommers, former Chief of Staff to John Boehner and President of the American Investment Council (the chief lobbyists for private equity), to David Rubenstein, billionaire private equity fund manager and so-called "patriotic philanthropist," the industry pushed back, and they won.

Against the will of the people and all common sense, the rich people with all the power successfully used their money and power to keep themselves as rich as they think they deserve.

Like I said before, it's the poster child for the corrupting influence of money in politics.

TOP MARGINAL TAX RATE

Corporate CEOs and private equity fund managers weren't the only wealthy Americans who benefited from the Republican tax plan, normal, everyday rich people who make a lot of money also came out on top.

In the process of changing personal income tax rates, the Republican tax bill cut the top tax rate for high income earners. It lowered the top rate from 39.6% to just 37%, and increased the point at which that rate starts from $428,400 for individuals and $470,700 for couples to over $500,000 for individuals and over $600,000 for couples.

This means that not only is the new top rate lower, less income is taxed at that top rate as well. **A 2.6% cut may not seem like much, but these members of the one percent are saving more than a minimum wage worker makes in a year.**

There's a common misconception that raising the top rate would hurt people in the upper middle class, but if you're making $500,000 a year, you're not in the middle class anymore

Final Trump-GOP Tax Bill Gives Larger Tax Cuts to Upper-Income Taxpayers in 2019 and Raises Taxes on Low-and Middle-Income Taxpayers in 2027

Tax Change as a Share of Income in 2019 and 2027, Includes Impact of ACA Individual Mandate Repeal

2019: 1.1%, 0.5%, 0.1%, -0.1%, -0.1%, -0.2%, -0.3%
2027: -0.7%, -1.3%, -1.5%, -1.6%, -1.8%, -3.5%, -2.7%

Poorest 20%, Second 20%, Middle 20%, Fourth 20%, Next 15%, Next 4%, Richest 1%

INSTITUTE ON TAXATION AND ECONOMIC POLICY • ITEP.ORG

While the Republican tax bill may offer tax cuts to everyone in the short run, in the long run the wealthy are the only ones who benefit in any significant way, if at all. The poor actually end up paying more.

no matter where you're living – you're in the top tier of Americans in terms of income. Even under the lower thresholds of the old tax code (the $428,400 number above), only the wealthiest one percent of Americans, less than one million households, made enough to qualify for the top rate.

I believe 37% is too low. 39.6% was too low too! No one wants to give up more of their income to the government, but no rich person, no matter how brilliant or talented, got there on their own, and we would do well to keep that in mind. We all benefited from investments made by those who preceded us, whether it was using technology that came as a result of

PATRIOTIC ▆ MILLIONAIRES
HOW TO THINK LIKE A PATRIOTIC MILLIONAIRE: TAXES

government research (like the Internet, which used to be called the Defense Advanced Research Project Agency Network), transporting our products on government–funded infrastructure, or even just going to public schools.

We made it because we lived in a society that was built to give us access to the American dream, but that opportunity is fading. How many amazing breakthroughs in science and technology are we missing out on because we don't tax the rich enough to properly fund scientific research? What if the next Apple won't ever happen because our young new Steve Jobs is stuck in an underfunded school system that never let him thrive? We're all worse off when opportunity is hoarded by those who've already succeeded. **So let the rich stay rich, but make them give back to the society that helped them get there, and pave the way for the next generation of innovators.**

HISTORICAL TAX RATES

We know that the wealthy can survive a higher income tax rate, because the current top income tax rate is actually one of the lowest we've seen in modern American history. Aside from a five year stretch in the late 80s and early 90s and the decade following the Bush tax cuts, the top marginal tax rate hasn't been below 38% since 1931.

In fact, during the 1940s, 50s, and 60s, decades of explosive economic growth in the United States, the top marginal tax rate never went
below 70 percent. For most of the 1950s, a decade seen by many as an economic golden age for the US, the top marginal tax rate was
91 percent. No one is advocating for a top income tax rate above 90 percent, but our own history proves beyond a shadow of a doubt that higher top income tax rates are not the economic poison their opponents claim them to be.

We can see the same principle at work not just in our past, but in the present as well. Most developed countries have significantly higher top rates than the United States, and their economies, for the most part, grow at the same general rate as the American economy.]

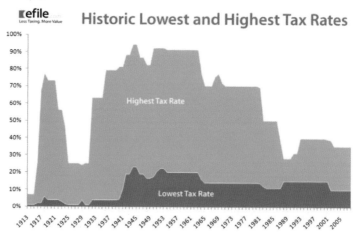

As you can see, the top marginal tax rate today is actually significantly lower than it has typically been in the last eighty years.

TAX BRACKETS

Someone making $550,000 a year in New York City is in a wildly different financial position than someone making $100 million a year in Kansas, yet our tax code treats their income as essentially the same. The difference between those two is much larger than the difference between that New Yorker and a regular member of the middle–class, **so why are they subject to the same tax rate?**

There's no legal constraint on Congress, it's simply a lack of political will to tax the ultra–rich. A more progressive system could have dozens of additional brackets that ensure as an individual's income continues to increase, that additional income is taxed at progressively higher rates. Income above $100 million could be taxed at a higher rate than income between $90 and $100 million, which is taxed higher than income between $80 and $90 million, and so on. **Lowering the number of tax brackets, or getting rid of them altogether in the name of a flat tax, would do nothing towards "simplification" of the tax code.**

But the complicated parts of the tax code that we worry about have nothing to do with the number of brackets and everything to do with the vast array of loopholes that the donor class has worked hard to preserve. We live in an era of calculators and computers – **simple math doesn't make things more complicated, unclear and ambiguous laws do.**

No one hires an accountant because they can't figure out what tax bracket they're in. Even in a world where the tax code had 500,000 brackets, it would still be as simple as inputting in your income into a website or spreadsheet and being told your bracket, no calculations required. **By consolidating brackets in the name of simplification, conservatives are really arguing for tax cuts for the wealthy.**

Limiting the number of brackets, or getting rid of them entirely, would give the wealthy a sizable tax cut and raise taxes on the middle–class at the same time. Doing the opposite, increasing the number of brackets (especially at the top), would ensure the ultra–wealthy end up paying more in taxes each year.

It's perfectly fair to believe that the wealthy should pay less in taxes, but if that's your position **you should just say it**. Don't try to hide a tax cut in language about "simplifying" the tax code.

We expect every American who works for their money to pay taxes.

Virtually every working American pays income taxes because we all agree that we as a society have things we want to do, and someone has to pay for them. But some believe that not everyone should have to pay for them. Or more specifically, that the wealthy heirs of multi–million dollar fortunes shouldn't have to pay for them. For decades the estate tax has ensured that wealthy heirs should pay taxes on the money they inherit just like people who actually work for their money, but recently the estate tax has been **under attack**.

There's a dedicated group of ultra–wealthy donors who are willing to spend big money convincing lawmakers that the so–called "death tax" should be abolished. They couldn't work up the political force to completely repeal the estate tax in the tax bill, but they managed to double the exemption limit, the point at which the tax kicks in.

This means that wealthy heirs can now inherit twice as much money tax-free.

Backing up, the **estate tax** is a tax on money someone receives as an inheritance when their parents (or other people) die.

This 40% tax only kicks in, however, on anything above the exemption limit of **$11.2 million for an individual or $22.4 million for a married couple**, indexed to inflation (up from around $5.5 million for an individual and $11 million for a couple before the Republican tax bill).

These numbers are important to lay out because they mean that only the absolute richest of the rich will ever pay a cent in estate tax. People in the middle class may hear about the "death tax" and be worried that they won't be able to leave anything to their children and grandchildren, but unless they win the lottery on their deathbed there's no chance of that happening. In fact, even with the previous lower threshold of $11 million for couples, only 2 out of every 1,000 estates paid any estate tax at all.

That's **less than 5,000** in the entire United States in a typical year, a number that the nonpartisan Joint Committee on Taxation estimates will be lowered to just **1,800** under the new law.

Even those estates that do qualify almost never pay anything close to the 40% mark, because only money above the cutoff gets taxed. The first $11.2 million or $22.4 million come absolutely tax free.

You could inherit $22,400,001 and only pay 40 cents in estate tax.

THE FAMILY FARM MYTH

During the debate over the Republican tax bill, Rep. Kristi Noem spoke out, telling the tragic story of how, after her father's accidental death, her family was hounded by the IRS for the government's cut of his estate. She claimed that in their time of tragedy, her family was forced to either sell the land that had been in their family for generations, or do what they ended up doing and take out a loan to pay off the estate tax.

It's a sad story. But it's a lie.

We won't dive into the technical details, but after some digging into

USA TODAY

She's the poster child for estate tax repeal, but her sad family saga doesn't add up

her story, journalists found that things simply didn't add up. It didn't make sense within the framework of the actual law, it only worked in a fantasy land in which the estate tax is an attack on family farms and small businesses. It isn't.

Let's look at the facts.

Almost no small business or family farm is worth enough to qualify for the estate tax at all, and those few that are pay much less than 40%.

In 2017, the owners of only about 80 small business or farms in the entire United States owed any estate tax at all. You can bet that number goes down even more with the higher exemption limit. Those that did paid, on average, less than 6% of their value in estate tax. So the owners of 80 small businesses had to pay a 6% tax after inheriting over $11 million worth of money and assets each. That hardly seems like an insidious plot to destroy the family farm.

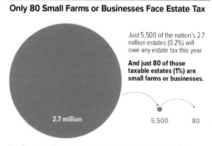
Only 80 Small Farms or Businesses Face Estate Tax

Just 5,500 of the nation's 2.7 million estates (0.2%) will owe any estate tax this year.

And just 80 of those taxable estates (1%) are small farms or businesses.

2.7 million   5,500   80

Note: The area of each pie is scaled to the number of estates. Small farms or businesses are estates whose farm and business assets total no more than $5 million and represent at least half of their gross value.

The estate tax is important because it is the **only** tax in the United States which is levied on some of the richest people in America. Most workers pay taxes on their income, but the rich don't have more income than regular people – they may actually have less.

I haven't actually worked for years, and I live off of my investments, so I have very little "income." The children of billionaires may never earn a
cent of "income" in their lives. The estate tax is the only tax which some of the richest people in this country will ever pay, and it is essential to ensure that they pay some semblance of their fair share of taxes.

Limiting it doesn't help middle–class Americans, or create jobs, or boost the economy. It does nothing more than give more money to the children of the rich, who already inherit millions without paying a cent of tax. One of the starkest differences between the two sides is that one believes that our country should only tax people who work for their income – and that the children of the rich, who inherit money and who have never worked a day in their life, should not pay any taxes. I believe that those of us who receive millions of dollars should pay taxes on that whether that money is from labor, from investments, or from wealth accumulated by our parents.

"If you want to see a world without the estate tax, you only have to look at England in the 19th century and before. You will see a permanent, entitled upper class who held a monopoly on wealth and a lower class trapped in poverty and servitude. Moving up economically was virtually impossible and those at the top considered themselves to be superior to everyone else which gave them the "right" to treat those less fortunate as though they were not human. The argument could be made that the vast majority of the people who came to these shores in the past 400 years, did so to escape this situation. They came for opportunity. The opportunity to succeed economically that was denied to them in their homelands. It was denied because of inherited wealth which prevented a level playing field.

Some of the most successful people in our history, would not have had the opportunity if this country allowed the unfettered flow of wealth from one generation to the next.

We are, and always have been, the land of opportunity. Nothing threatens that more than the repeal of the estate tax."

– Bob Haines, Patriotic Millionaire

STEPPED-UP BASIS

There's an even bigger tax break for the children of wealthy parents than raising the estate tax exemption limit, and it's one that doesn't get talked about a lot. It's called the stepped–up basis.

The stepped–up basis is a tax benefit for people inheriting assets instead of money (which is often the case for the ultra–rich, they rarely keep their fortunes in cash) that allows families to completely avoid paying capital gains taxes on those assets.

Normally, long term capital gains taxes are assessed on increases in the value of an asset. So if you bought a bundle of stocks worth $50 million a few years ago and then sold it for $90 million, you would have to pay taxes on that gain of $40 million. But what if you didn't sell those stocks? You only pay capital gains taxes when you sell your assets, not
when their value goes up. If you don't sell the stocks, you don't pay taxes on them. That's all totally reasonable.

The problem arises, however, when someone with a lot of assets dies and passes those assets down to their heirs. Rather than continue to treat the "basis," or starting price of the asset, at where it was when it was first purchased, the basis is "stepped up" for the heirs, meaning that for the purposes of their sale of the asset, the original value is whatever it was when they inherited it. So if you passed along that $90 million bundle of stocks to your heirs (which has increased in value by $40 million without you paying any taxes on it), and they then sold it for $110 million a few years later, they would only pay taxes on $20 million in gains, not $60 million.

This means all of that increase in value will go to that family without anyone ever paying taxes on it.

Pictured is the Mars Family, with a combined net worth of $60 billion

This little piece of the tax code has massive implications. Some of the wealthiest families in America have huge amounts of assets that have never been and will never be taxed. Sam Walton never paid taxes on the increased value of his ownership stake in Walmart from zero to tens of billions of dollars, and now his children (and his son–in–law) are five of the twenty richest people in the world, and no one ever paid one penny of taxes on the vast majority of that vast accumulation of wealth. Same with the Mars family (three more of the richest billionaires in the world are the children of Forrest Mars, who created the Mars candy fortune), and a number of others. We're losing out on billions in tax revenue because these billionaires managed to convince Congress that it was unfair for their kids to pay taxes on what they inherited, never mind that they got it all for free anyway.

FIGURE 4

Step-up in basis primarily benefits the wealthy
Share of total tax benefits

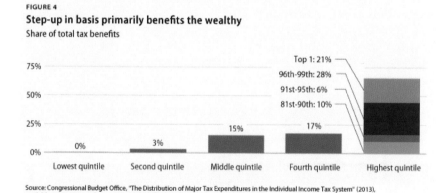

Source: Congressional Budget Office, "The Distribution of Major Tax Expenditures in the Individual Income Tax System" (2013), available at http://www.cbo.gov/sites/default/files/cbofiles/attachments/43768_DistributionTaxExpenditures.pdf.

The top 10% of Americans get almost all of the benefits of the stepped–up basis. Image credit to the Center for American Progress

1031 EXCHANGE

The carried interest loophole is just one a dozens of payouts to certain industries, another one is 1031 exchanges. 1031 exchanges, or "like– kind" exchanges, are a gimmick in the tax code that benefits wealthy real estate developers (like the one currently sitting in the Oval Office). They particularly benefit their children, by working in sync with the stepped– up basis.

A like–kind exchange means that a real estate developer who sells one of his properties is able to avoid paying taxes on any gains in the value of that property as long as it's reinvested in a similar property. This means that a developer like Donald Trump or Jared Kushner could sell one of their buildings, buy another building with the money from that sale, and keep doing so over and over without ever paying a cent of tax. When combined with the stepped–up basis, this means that families with extensive real estate holdings can avoid paying taxes on their properties indefinitely.

Jared Kushner's property at 666 5th avenue, New York, NY

CONCLUSION

The Patriotic Millionaires, like most Americans, know that our citizens should have a tax code that does what it's supposed to do – pays for what we need and shares those costs fairly. Like most Americans, we want a tax code that will build the middle class, create good jobs, grow the economy, reward productive citizens and companies, and invest in our future.

But it's clear that not every millionaire wants that kind of tax code. Many of those *other millionaires* want to live in a country with a tiny number of rich people, millions of poor people and no middle class, and they've been spending millions to write the rules of our economy to lead to that result.

But unlike *those* millionaires, we don't want to pretend we made our money in Ireland, or get out of paying taxes because we were born rich and never had to work, or take advantage of tax breaks for long term investors because we advise long term investors. And we sure as hell don't want to pay lower tax rates than the people who work for us.

It's not because we are nice or good or altruistic, it's because we think that is the only way to create the kind of country we want to live in. We want to live in a country where hard work is rewarded. Where good businesses thrive. Where people feel safe in their neighborhoods. Where parents can tell their children that they're going to be okay — and really believe it. We want to live in a country that has a basic sense of fairness, and where millionaires don't get special treatment just because they're rich.

Those *other* millionaires? They want special treatment. They honestly believe that they *deserve* special treatment. They puff up their chests, call themselves "Job Creators" and insist the economy will collapse if (god forbid!) they are asked to pay a single penny more in taxes.

Nonsense. Millionaires put their pants on one leg at a time, just like everyone else. Consumer demand is the only real "job creator." And nothing is going to collapse if millionaires pay their fair share (except for possibly an over– inflated ego or two).

I wrote this book in the hopes that some of my fellow citizens – those who are millionaires and those who are not, people in both parties and no party at all – will read it and be inspired to think differently about taxes. Then I hope they will act.

TOGETHER WE CAN BUILD THE NEXT BEST CENTURY FOR OUR NATION.